AND THE WINNER IS

BY MITCH ALBOM

★

★

DRAMATISTS
PLAY SERVICE
INC.

AND THE WINNER IS
Copyright © 2008, Mitch Albom

All Rights Reserved

SPECIAL NOTE

SPECIAL NOTE ON SONGS AND RECORDINGS

AND THE WINNER IS was originally produced by The Purple Rose Theatre Company (Jeff Daniels, Executive Director; Guy Sanville, Artistic Director; Alan Ribant, Managing Director) in Chelsea, Michigan, opening on June 23, 2005. It was directed by Guy Sanville; the set design was by Vincent Mountain; the costume design was by Christianne Myers; the lighting design was by Reid G. Johnson; the sound design was by Quintessa Gallinat; and the stage manager was Michelle DiDomenico. The cast was as follows:

TYLER JOHNES .... Grant R. Krause
SEAMUS .... Paul Hopper
TEDDY LaPETITE .... Wayne David Parker
KYLE MORGAN .... Patrick Michael Kenney
SHERI .... Sarab Kamoo
SERENITY .... Jerri Doll

CHARACTERS

TYLER JOHNES — mid-40s, actor

SEAMUS — late 60s/70ish, white beard, impish, Irish, bartender

TEDDY LaPETITE — late 30s/40ish, French, agent

KYLE MORGAN — late 20s, handsome, actor

SHERI — late 30s, Tyler's wife

SERENITY — early 20s, bombshell, actress

PLACE

Act One takes place in a mythical Irish bar somewhere between here and heaven.

Act Two takes place at the Academy Awards.

TIME

Now.

AND THE WINNER IS

ACT ONE

Darkness. Music up. A song like The Crests' "Trouble in Paradise."* As it fades, the sound of harsh winds blowing. Then a man's deep breath. In. Out. In. Out. Lights up on Seamus, an old Irishman, who sits atop a stool in what seems to be a dilapidated bar. A large open chute is on the back wall. Seamus is reading a magazine. He has a stack of them on the bar. He sings to himself.

SEAMUS.
Tu-ra-lu-ra-lu-ral
tu-ra-lu-ra-li …
(As he continues, a single child's voice is heard.)
CHILD. *(Offstage.)*
Now I lay me down to sleep, I pray
the lord my soul to keep.
(As that voice continues, another starts.)
CHILD 2.
Now I lay me down to sleep …
(Then another, then another, until quickly there are hundreds of voices, children and adults, overlapping. Seamus continues singing. It all grows to a crescendo:)
SEAMUS.
… tu-ra lu-ra lu-ral …
VOICES.
Now I lay me down to sleep,
I pray the lord my soul to keep …
If I should die before I wake …
before I wake … before I wake …
SEAMUS. 'Tis an Irish lullabye! *(The sound of a train. Then a*

* See Special Note on Songs and Recordings on copyright page.

5

scream, ending it all.)

TYLER. *(Offstage.)* Arrhhhhhh! *(Suddenly, with a loud rumbling sound, Tyler Johnes comes tumbling out of the chute and lands in the center of the floor. He is wearing boxer shorts, one sock, and a semibuttoned dress shirt, as if he fell asleep undressing.)* Arhhhhhhh! *(He's writhing. Seamus tries to ignore him. Moaning now.)* Arrrhhhh ... ahhhh ... (Seamus looks up, annoyed that his reading is interrupted. He takes a seltzer bottle, approaches Tyler, and sprays it all over his face.)* Whooooa! Hey! *(Coming to.)* What was that for? *(No response. Seamus returns to the table. Looking around:)* Man, I must've drunk half the vodka in ... Hey. This isn't Hailey's ... Jesus, where am I? *(At the word "Jesus," Seamus takes a small clicker from his pocket and, without looking up, clicks it once. Tyler is jolted as if by electric shock.)* Ow! ... What was that? ... Christ! *(Seamus clicks again. Another jolt.)* Ow! ... Jesus! *(Another click. Same thing.)* Where are my PANTS? *(Stopping to laugh at himself.)* Hmmph. This'll make a great story in *Variety* tomorrow. *(Imagining it.)* "Tyler Johnes began the morning on the floor of a bar without his pants. By evening, he was the toast of Hollywood." *(Proud of himself.)* What do you think?

SEAMUS. *(Without looking up.)* Nice undies.

TYLER. Rainman speaks! I'll be goddamned. *(Another click. Another flop. Tyler stays down, assumes mock lotus position. Chanting quickly.)* Ommmm! Ommmmm!

SEAMUS. What's that you're doing?

TYLER. Meditation. My guru taught me, Swami Shakapukapanda. Ommmm! Supposed to calm me down. Ommmm! *(Gives up.)* Shit, it's not working. *(Rises to mirror.)* I LOOK LIKE CRAP! JESUS! *(Another click by Seamus. Another jolt.)* Ow! ... And my chest is killing me.

SEAMUS. *(Lowering the magazine.)* It wasn't exactly your chest. Technically it was a "major myocardial infarction," what my ma used to call "putting your ticker crossways" and what is known in your parlance, I believe, as "a freakin' heart attack." *(He returns to his magazine.)*

TYLER. Where are my PANTS!?

SEAMUS. *(Again lowers magazine.)* I'm not gonna finish this, am I? OK. Here we go. Listen carefully. *(Inhales, then quickly, a standard speech.)* You're dead, you died, you passed over, you croaked, thy kingdom come, His will be done, forever and ever — shave and a haircut, two bits — amen.

TYLER. Oh, my God.

SEAMUS. You're getting it.

TYLER. Oh, my God!

SEAMUS. NOW you're getting it —

TYLER. Tonight's the Oscars, and I don't have my tux!

SEAMUS. You're not getting it.

TYLER. Oh, yes I am! I'm getting that tux! *(Moving around, looking.)* Where's your phone? The red carpet starts at four o'clock.

SEAMUS. I'm afraid there'll be no red carpet.

TYLER. Shit no, not without a tux! Look, Lucky Charms man? I need a phone, OK? Teddy is probably freaking out.

SEAMUS. Teddy?

TYLER. Teddy LaPetite. My agent. A giant in the business.

SEAMUS. LaPetite?

TYLER. I need a phone!

SEAMUS. So you're an actor then?

TYLER. *(Measuring him.)* You're kidding, right? Hello? I'm Tyler Johnes!

SEAMUS. I knew an actor once. A terrible drunk. Couldn't keep his wig on straight.

TYLER. Arrrgh! ... What kind of bar doesn't have a phone? Or ... *(Looking around.)* ... a cigarette machine ... or liquor?

SEAMUS. The liquor I miss. So! An actor. A grand life it must be, on the stage.

TYLER. Are you nuts? Live theater is for losers. I'm Tyler Johnes. Movie star?

SEAMUS. Why did you call me the Lucky Charms man?

TYLER. Say "They're magically delicious."

SEAMUS. They're magically delicious.

TYLER. That's why. *(Sudden sound of a train speeding past. Tyler looks up, around. Seamus is nonplussed.)* What's that, a train?

SEAMUS. No. Just the sound of one.

TYLER. I pass out one night, and L.A. gets mass transit ... ARRG! TYLER, YOU IDIOT! A hangover before the Oscars? I gotta call Christine.

SEAMUS. Your wife?

TYLER. My makeup artist. *(Chants frantically, closes eyes.)* Ommm. Ommm ... SHIT! IT'S NOT WORKING! Jesus, that guru SUCKS! *(Another click, another flop. Seamus returns to his magazines. Tyler realizes he needs his help. Decides to charm him.)*

OK. Let's start over *(Holds out hand.)* Your name is … *(Seamus looks up. Takes his hand.)*

SEAMUS. Seamus.

TYLER. Lovely name. I'm Tyler Johnes. *(They shake.)* With an H. J-o-h-n-e-s.

SEAMUS. Ah.

TYLER. My agent's idea.

SEAMUS. The H?

TYLER. And the Johnes. My real name is Steinberg.

SEAMUS. He gave you a new last name, and then he changed the spelling?

TYLER. I told you he was good.

SEAMUS. *(Considering.)* Tyler Steinberg.

TYLER. Jake.

SEAMUS. Jake?

TYLER. He gave me the Tyler, too.

SEAMUS. Jake.

TYLER. Jacob, actually.

SEAMUS. You're making me dizzy, lad.

TYLER. Jacob Steinberg! Would you keep that name in Hollywood? It sounds like you're building a kibbutz.

SEAMUS. You're Jewish then?

TYLER. *(Sarcastically.)* Uh … duh!

SEAMUS. I admire Jewish people. They're like the Irish. Every couple of centuries, they get the crap kicked out of them.

TYLER. Well, that's fascinating. Now, a phone? — *(Another train sound. Tyler looks but barely stops.)* — This is only, like, the most important day of my life.

SEAMUS. *(Showing new interest.)* Why is that? Are you taking a bride? Is a baby being born?

TYLER. The Oscars! Hello? I'm nominated! Best Supporting Actor? *The Wind and the Fury?* Hello? … Why am I talking to you?

SEAMUS. I'm the only one here. Now. Let's prioritize … *The Wind and the Fury?*

TYLER. That's the movie.

SEAMUS. A talkie?

TYLER. *(Exasperated.)* Yes. A talkie.

SEAMUS. And you were in it?

TYLER. *(Going to sit down.)* I got nominated, for Christ's sake! *(Another click by Seamus. Tyler grabs his rear end in pain.)* Finally!

I'm forty-six. Don't say anything, but I am. Forty-six.

SEAMUS. *(Sadly, as if mourning.)* Such a young man.

TYLER. Not in Hollywood. At forty-six, they're fitting you for Depends ... All those bullshit films when I was younger. Don't get me wrong, I dug the whole *Chippin-Cop* franchise.

SEAMUS. Chippen-Cop?

TYLER. Hello? Tyler Johnes in *Chippen-Cop, Chippen-Cop II, Chippen-Cop III, Another Chippen-Cop* and *Chippin-Cop Academy*? It was a franchise. You don't fart at a franchise.

SEAMUS. *(Amused.)* No. You don't fart at a franchise.

TYLER. Tell me you never saw those films. Cops by day, Chippendales strippers at night? Tyler Johnes and Kyle Morgan — the Chippin-Cops? Sexy and Sassy? I was Sassy. *(Enter Kyle, dream-like, with gun, doing TV cop poses as he moves across the stage. Tyler regards him, moves with him, mocking him.)*

SEAMUS. Who's the other fellow?

TYLER. My co-star. Kyle Morgan. Asshole.

SEAMUS. With an h?

TYLER. Oh, yeah. A-s-s — big stinkin' H — hole. We were friends for awhile.

SEAMUS. And then?

TYLER. He stole my wife.

SEAMUS. Oh. *(Exit Kyle.)*

TYLER. *(Back to Seamus.)* It went downhill from there.

SEAMUS. I see. *(Lights up on Sheri, Tyler's wife, in a memory moment.)*

SHERI. I see. *(Tyler spins to her.)*

TYLER. You see me leaving, is what you see.

SHERI. You have to live here to leave here, Jake.

TYLER. I live here.

SHERI. You shower here.

TYLER. Not anymore! I wouldn't want to burst in on you, Kyle, and soap on a rope!

SHERI. Nothing happened! And you're not being fair. Admit it. You've been running around on me like crazy.

TYLER. I don't know what you're talking about.

SHERI. Oh, no? Pick any night of the week. Your Monday girl. Your Tuesday girl —

TYLER. You're the one with a guy in the bed —

SHERI. I can't believe you're trying to flip this on me! All I ever did was love you — and wait for you to come home.

TYLER. Hey, it wasn't me who packed ten pounds on your rear end.

SHERI. *(Flabbergasted.)* Ohhh … so … so, what, you can do whatever you want if I don't make my weight?

TYLER. Spare me the self-pity. Where's your gratitude? I've made your life a thousand times better.

SHERI. Who ARE you? … The way you've treated me since you became …

TYLER. A star? Is that too much for you to handle, Sher?

SHERI. *(Fighting tears.)* I was going to ask *you* that question.

TYLER. Don't bother. I'm leaving. You and Kyle have fun!

SHERI. You DON'T … UNDERSTAND.

TYLER. I'm leaving! And you'll regret it! You hear me? —

SHERI. *(Clutching him, they fall to their knees.)* Jake! No! I love you! I love you! Don't go!

TYLER. I will never come back here! *(Sheri rises and exits. Tyler bangs the floor, alone.)* Nevermore! Nevermore! NEVERMORE! *(A beat. Tyler snaps out of it as if it never happened.)* Anyhow, the Chippen-Cops was a franchise, and you don't fart at a franchise. Although I never liked being the Sassy one. I mean, who would? Kyle Morgan. Sexy. Tyler Johnes, Sassy. Ugh. Talk about shitty billing.

SEAMUS. Tyler —

TYLER. These young actors — they're like locusts! I gotta do botox and tanning booths. He rolls out of bed all bronzed and smooth, like a goddamm Pillsbury biscuit. *(A click. A flop.)* Anyhow, that all changes if I win this Oscar. They judge you on your performance, you know.

SEAMUS. Boyo, I need to clear up your situation here —

TYLER. *(Animated.)* Wanna hear how it happened? Here's how it happened! I told Teddy "Enough Chippen-Cops!" Make me blind!

SEAMUS. You asked to be blind?

TYLER. Blind. Deaf. Dumb. That's how you win an Oscar.

SEAMUS. Listen, Tyler-Jake-Jacob —

TYLER. And then, out of the blue, *The Wind and the Fury*, a small art flick, right? They got this guy in it — "serious" actor, nothing but Circle Rep and Royal Shakespeare and PBS Playhouse and all that nonpaying shit — and he's playing this gimpy Civil War courier, one legged, partially blind, speech impediment.

SEAMUS. Oh, my.

TYLER. I know! Jackpot! So this Circle Rep guy, two days before shooting … he drops out! *He drops out!* A gastric ulcer! Serves him right. All that Richard the Third.

SEAMUS. Aye! I know that one! Richard the Third. "Now is the winter of our discontent — "

TYLER. *(Joining Seamus.)* " … winter of our discontent, made glorious summer by this Duke of York." Yeah, yeah, yeah. So … he drops out, goes back to Woodstock with his Shakespeare and his Maalox, and Teddy gets me into *The Wind and the Fury* — at a reduced rate, I might add — and I play the one legged Civil War courier with the bad eye and the speech impediment and I play the SHIT out of that part, great reviews and NO box office — the critics love that, it's like they're adopting a puppy — and then, last month, the morning of the nominations, I get that call at five-thirty A.M.

SEAMUS. A phone call, this is? —

TYLER. *(Not breaking stride.)* I pretended I was asleep. Everybody does. *(Mocking.)* "Oh, I completely forgot it was Oscar day." BulllllSHIT! There isn't an actor on the planet who isn't staring at the phone by four A.M.! I, personally, had to take two Valiums just to get through the night.

SEAMUS. Valiums?

TYLER. You don't have any, do you?

SEAMUS. I doubt it —

TYLER. So anyhow, sure enough, five-thirty, the phone rings.

SEAMUS. Good news!

TYLER. No. It was my wife. *(Lights up on Sheri. Memory moment. She's holding phone. Tyler snorts cocaine.)*

SHERI. Jake, I need to talk to you.

TYLER. Sheri! Get off my line! IT'S OSCAR NOMINATION MORNING!

SHERI. But you won't pick up —

TYLER. I haven't got time for your little problems right now.

SHERI. You're not God, Jake Steinberg.

TYLER. And you're not the Academy. So hang up!

SHERI. But I need to share something with —

TYLER. Share it with Kyle! *(He hangs up. Lights off on Sheri. Tyler as if it never happened, turns back to Seamus.)* It was my wife.

SEAMUS. But I thought she left you for Morgan.

TYLER. Use his first name: Ass clown. And she didn't leave me. I left her. I haven't signed the divorce papers on account of I'm not giving her all the satisfaction AND half the stuff! So we're "technically" still married. *(Off his look.)* What? In California, that's considered a healthy relationship.

SEAMUS. She still calls you?

TYLER. Let her beg.

SEAMUS. She still loves you?

TYLER. Too late! You gotta play it straight if you wanna play with Tyler Johnes — know what I mean?

SEAMUS. I haven't a clue.

TYLER. Anyhow, ever since the nomination, everything's changed! I'm getting calls from people who last year wouldn't say God bless you if I sneezed.

SEAMUS. Do you do that?

TYLER. Do what?

SEAMUS. Say "God bless you" when someone sneezes?

TYLER. Shit, no! I don't talk to strangers!

SEAMUS. *(Disappointed.)* Too bad. It might have helped.

TYLER. So, anyhow, that's my E Entertainment story — for the moment. And now, my good fellow, if you would fetch me my pants. And a cab. *(He waits, as if Seamus is his servant.)* A cab? A town car? A limo? A stretch? An SUV? A hummer? A helicopter? A — *(Lights change. He looks to the outer windows.)* Hey, look at all those people. Are they lining up for the red carpet already? *(Checks watch.)* My watch is dead. Jesus! *(A click. A flop. Tyler stays down. Seamus stands behind him.)*

SEAMUS. I need to tell you something. Some take it better than others. *(Beat.)* I have a feeling you're gonna vomit.

TYLER. What is it, old man? You hard up? If you fix me a drink I can give you a few bucks —

SEAMUS. *(Pointedly.)* Shut it now, lad! I am not your bloody barkeep. *(Sighing, calming down.)* You died. In your sleep. Your heart attacked you. You came down the hatch and now you're here.

TYLER. *(Playing along.)* Um-hmmm … OK. So I'm dead.

SEAMUS. Affirmative.

TYLER. And this is where you go when you're dead.

SEAMUS. This is where YOU go.

TYLER. Ah. I see. My eternal rest is a bar with no cigarettes, no phone and … no beer!

SEAMUS. Aye.

TYLER. I can't wait to see where you send Kyle Morgan. I played the *good* cop. *(Chants quickly.)* Ommmm! Ommmm! Come on, old man. A dry bar? Even God can't have that cruel a sense of humor.

SEAMUS. *(Glumly.)* … You'd be surprised.

TYLER. Prove it.

SEAMUS. Well, do you remember that little prayer, "Now I lay me down to sleep, I pray the lord my soul to keep"?

TYLER. *(Disinterested.)* Yeah?

SEAMUS. You didn't say it.

TYLER. I didn't say it when?

SEAMUS. The night you croaked. And that's why you're here.

TYLER. I'm here because I didn't say my lines?

SEAMUS. Aye.

TYLER. And where do the lucky people who *did* say it go?

SEAMUS. *(Pointing to window.)* There.

TYLER. The lucky people who say it go to the Oscars?

SEAMUS. Not the Oscars, boyo. Heaven. Valhalla. Shangri La. Abraham's bosom.

TYLER. So this isn't heaven.

SEAMUS. It's … a way station.

TYLER. IIIII … gotcha.

SEAMUS. Good.

TYLER. NOW can I phone my agent?

SEAMUS. Arrrgh! You're dead, boyo! Don't you get it? There's no phone! Jiminy Peters, you're giving me a headache.

TYLER. You get headaches in heaven?

SEAMUS. Aye.

TYLER. Can you get aspirin?

SEAMUS. I said he has a cruel sense of humor.

TYLER. Right … Look, Mister. I appreciate this whole charade. It's nice work. Community theater, maybe, but nice work. Now just open the back door, and I won't press charges. *(Seamus contemplates something.)*

SEAMUS. I don't like to get physical.

TYLER. *(Laughing.)* What? You're gonna beat me up? OK … Bring it on, old man! *(Strikes karate pose.)* I did three karate movies in the eighties! Hyyyyuhh! *(Seamus stares at the silly pose. He gently takes one of Tyler's hands and places it on his chest.)*

SEAMUS. Feel … listen … *(Tyler goes from confused to slowly panicked. He moves his hand around his chest, then his rib cage. Softly:)* You have no heartbeat … because it's not beating anymore …

TYLER. *(As it starts to register.)* I … died…?

13

SEAMUS. You took the big dirt nap.

TYLER. No … No-ho-ho-ho! … *(Rising.)* No! *(Runs in a circle.)* No-no-no-no-no-no-no-no-no NOOOOOOOO! NO-NO-NOOOOOOO!

SEAMUS. I KNEW you wouldn't like it.

TYLER. NOBODY DIES THE NIGHT BEFORE THE OSCARS! YOU MISS ALL THE PARTIES!

SEAMUS. We're not on the same schedule up here.

TYLER. NO-NO-NO-NO-NO! I HAVE A FREAKING LIMOUSINE AT FREAKING FOUR-THIRTY! I HAVE A GIRLFRIEND HALF MY AGE WITH A LOW CUT DRESS AND A GREAT ASS THAT I HAVE BEEN KEEPING FOR JUST THIS OCCASION!

SEAMUS. The dress?

TYLER. THE ASS! *(Starts chanting again, frantically.)* Ommm! Ommmm! I AM GOING TO THE OSCARS WITH THAT GIRL AND HER GREAT ASS OH, YEAH, I AM GOING TO THE OSCARS IF IT KILLS ME!

SEAMUS. It's a little late for —

TYLER. Don't say it! Don't say another … goddamn word. *(Another click. Flop. Seamus returns to his seat and his magazine. Tyler senses an escape. He slowly crawls towards the hatch door. When he's close enough, he rises.)* Bye bye! *(He runs to the hatch. A huge burst of light explodes from it. He falls backwards in pain.)*

SEAMUS. That's going to cost you.

TYLER. *(Still stunned.)* Cost me what?

SEAMUS. Time.

TYLER. How much time?

SEAMUS. On your calender? Four hundred years.

TYLER. What! That's insane! We don't give four hundred years to serial killers!

SEAMUS. Why don't you make the most of it? Read something.

TYLER. Read? What should I READ, old man? The Holy Bible? The Greatest Story Ever Told? *(Seamus grabs a magazine from the stack and offers it.)*

SEAMUS. *Highlights*!

TYLER. *Highlights*?

SEAMUS. It's all we get here. It's a children's magazine. They have these little puzzles on the back page —

TYLER. I know what *Highlights* is! FOR THE LOVE OF GOD

14

THIS CAN'T BE HAPPENING! NOBODY DIES THE NIGHT BEFORE THE OSCARS! Look, Mister. There's gotta be some way to get me back!

SEAMUS. Get you back?

TYLER. For one night. Please! Let me get my tux, go to the Oscars — and then I'll come back here! Scout's honor! You can have me for four hundred years! Five hundred years!

SEAMUS. You'd wait another hundred years just to see if you won an award?

TYLER. It's not just an award! It's THE award! It means I was good!

SEAMUS. You don't need others to tell you you were good. *(Looks up.)* He'll take care of that.

TYLER. Please? ... PUH-LEEEEZE? *(Beat.)*

SEAMUS. Ahhh. I don't know ...

TYLER. Come on! Look at us! We have no booze in our bar! I could pick up some of my old friends, Mr. Jack Daniels, Mr. Jim Beam. It's like running to the Seven-Eleven. No one's watching!

SEAMUS. *(Ruefully.)* ... Someone's always watching, boyo. *(Tyler crosses to corner. Drops. Buries face in hands. Starts to cry. Weeping. Wailing. Overdone acting. He peeks through his fingers to see if it's having an effect. Seamus is moved. The more it seems like Seamus is considering it, the louder Tyler wails.)* All right, all right. Stop your whining.

TYLER. *(Thrilled.)* You can do it? I can go back?

SEAMUS. Aye. But whatever happens, you can't look away.

TYLER. Scout's honor!

SEAMUS. No matter what.

TYLER. When do we leave?

SEAMUS. Down on your knees. *(Tyler drops.)* Close your eyes.

TYLER. Eyes are closed!

SEAMUS. Think hard if this is what you really want, boyo.

TYLER. It is, it is, it is! *(Train sound. Then a rumbling from the wall. Tyler opens his eyes. Teddy La Petite, Tyler's agent, comes tumbling out of the chute and lands before Tyler's outstretched arms. A short, tense man, Teddy is wearing pajamas.)*

TEDDY. Arrrgh! *(Tyler rises, encircles him, stares in disbelief.)* Arrrrgh! ARRRRGH! *(Seamus, as if doing a monotonous chore, picks up the seltzer bottle, steps over. Tyler looks at him. Seamus sprays the seltzer in Teddy's face. Calming down:)* Ooohh ... ooophhh ... Jesus

15

... *(Seamus clicks as he resumes his seat. Teddy flops over.)*

TYLER. *(Half-whisper.)* I don't believe it ... Teddy? *(Teddy looks up at him.)*

TEDDY. *(Weakly, full of hope.)* Tyler? ...

TYLER. Teddy, why didn't you tell me about this "now I lay me down to sleep" shit?

TEDDY. Tyler? ...

TYLER. *(Crossing to Seamus.)* Hey, hey, what gives? I asked to go back, and you send me my agent? In his PAJAMAS? What's he gonna do? Cut the deal? *(Suddenly dawns on him.)* Teddy! Get up! You gotta cut a deal. *(He lifts the dazed Teddy and pushes him in front of Seamus.)*

TEDDY. Where am I? I feel so strange ...

TYLER. Say hello to Father Flanagan.

TEDDY. *(Dazed.)* Hello, Father.

SEAMUS. It's Seamus.

TYLER. And this is Teddy.

SEAMUS. *(Eyeing his height.)* The giant. *(Teddy reaches into his pajama pocket, pulls out a card, offers it weakly. Taking card.)* Ahh ... 'S. Theodore LaPetite.

TYLER. *(Correcting him.)* Teddy.

SEAMUS. *(Lightly scolding.)* Jacob.

TEDDY. *(Turning.)* Jacob?

SEAMUS. Teddy.

TEDDY. *(Turning back.)* Seamus?

TYLER. Jesus! *(Clicked.)* Ow!

SEAMUS. I need to tell you something.

TYLER. *(Exasperated.)* Here we go!

SEAMUS. You've passed over. You died. You left your mortal life behind.

TEDDY. You know, I have felt a bit peaked since I got — *(Suddenly hits him.)* I WHAT? I WHAT? MORTE? I AM DEAD?

TYLER. Get a grip. You act like nothing bad ever happened to you before.

TEDDY. No, Impossible! I am not prepared to expire! I have meetings all day long! Jesus! *(A click. A flop.)* The clicking, what is the clicking? WHERE AM I?

SEAMUS. It's a way station, laddy.

TYLER. The ass end of eternity.

SEAMUS. You wait here for an opening to proceed on your destiny —

TYLER. And the good news is … it'll only take four hundred years!

TEDDY. *(Totally confused, trying to take control.)* All right … My client has clearly been drugged. And nobody drugs TYLER JOHNES! Except Tyler Johnes. Monsieur Seamus, I must warn you, you are facing criminal charges. Entrapment … Reckless endangerment!

SEAMUS. *(Weary, grabbing magazine.)* Theodore. Have you ever read *Highlights*?

TYLER. Teddy! Call him Teddy! … Now look, Teddy. I died in my sleep. What about you? What's the last thing you remember?

TEDDY. *(Pacing.)* We were at Hailey's. We were eating. You were there. Your girlfriend, Serenity … I had the "Tower of Shellfish."

SEAMUS. The what?

TEDDY. It's a specialty. The "Tower of Shellfish:" shrimp, lobster, mussels, and clams, stacked high on a big stick, doused in a white wine sauce, tres delicieux, and very reasonably priced —

TYLER. TEDDY!

TEDDY. Anyhow, we went home, a la maison, I felt a bit queasy … Wait. Mon Dieu! *(Click, flop.)* Tyler. You're dead, too?

TYLER. Mmm-hmmm. *(Teddy runs across and squeezes him.)*

TEDDY. WHY LORD, WHY? *(Break, he slaps Tyler.)* Tyler! We had that development deal at Paramount! And your *Chippen-Cop* residuals! And your divorce, ach, merde, I TOLD you to sign your divorce papers. If you are dead, your wife, she gets everything! This SUCKS the big one! *(He removes a blackberry, starts typing.)* I will email the bank.

TYLER. You keep a blackberry in your pajamas?

TEDDY. Mais, oui.

TYLER. *(To Seamus.)* I thought they say, "You can't take it with you."

SEAMUS. Nonsense. You can take anything you want. But it won't do you much good.

TEDDY. He's right. The battery is dead.

SEAMUS. Do you ever pray, Theodore?

TYLER. Yeah, Teddy. Did you ever say that prayer, "Now I lay me down to sleep"?

TEDDY. Non.

TYLER. See! You guys need to update the rules!

TEDDY. WHY AM I HERE?

TYLER. You forgot to say the magic words.

TEDDY. Gross, not net?

TYLER. I *TOLD* you he was good.

SEAMUS. You're in an in-between place, boyo. Had you asked the Lord your soul to keep, you'd be out there.

TEDDY. *(Looking through the glass.)* Hey ... that's Phil Nushki! He died last week! *(Bangs on window.)* Phil! Phil! I was at your funeral! *(Back to Tyler.)* That putz owes me two percent on a cable deal.

TYLER. All those people get to go before us?

SEAMUS. Aye. You wait for a lull.

TYLER and TEDDY. *(Mocking the pronunciation.)* A lull?

SEAMUS. A lull. In traffic.

TEDDY. Why do they go first?

SEAMUS. Because they asked. "I pray the Lord my soul to keep." He's very literal.

TYLER. Why didn't someone tell us?

SEAMUS. Tell you what? You learned the prayer as children. You're lucky it's so simple. The original prayer was *(Breaking into a chant.)* "kuntaya ghantyuna itysuissiui chhanh"!

TYLER. What the HELL is THAT?

SEAMUS. Aramaic. Dead language.

TYLER. God wanted us to pray in a dead language?

SEAMUS. Well, He thought heaven should be a *little* difficult!

TEDDY. I don't believe this!

SEAMUS. But then one night, somewhere in the world, a wee child was sick with the influenza. He was hot and sweating and deathly pale, and his mother feared he wouldn't last the night. So together they made up this little prayer — Now I lay me down to sleep — and when they finished he nodded off, like a little angel. And he died before he waked. And God took his soul, just as he asked. *(Beat.)*

TYLER. *(Annoyed.)* ANNND...?

SEAMUS. Precedent was set. No more Aramaic.

TEDDY. *(Glumly.)* We are doomed.

TYLER. *(Fast, hopefully.)* No, we're not doomed, Teddy ... nice Mr. Seamus can send us back.

TEDDY. That's goddamn great! *(Click. Flop.)*

SEAMUS. First, I'll need some details.

TYLER. Kodak Theater, corner of Highland and Hollywood —

SEAMUS. Not directions. Details. About you, Tyler Johnes, with an H.

TYLER. *(Pushing Teddy forward.)* Teddy handles the details. *(Seamus moves to the bar, picks up a clipboard and pen.)*

SEAMUS. I need to know … who has he helped?

TEDDY. *(Long beat.)* I'm not following.

SEAMUS. On earth … Who … has … he helped? Helped. With an H. *(Tyler laughs, as if this couldn't be simpler. Teddy joins him, the laughter growing from small chuckles to guffaws.)*

TEDDY. That's … I mean, that's far too easy …

TYLER. It's surprisingly … easy. *(Laughter fading.)*

TEDDY. Who's he helped? … Alors, where do we start, no? *(To Tyler.)* Where *do* we start?

TYLER. Come on, Teddy.

TEDDY. Welll … Tyler Johnes has helped many peoples along the way … *(Awkward pause.)*

SEAMUS. You can name me one.

TYLER. *(Suddenly remembering.)* Wait, wait! That charity party! At Keisha's. For Africa? "Save the industrious peoples."

TEDDY. The *indigenous* peoples.

TYLER. Yeah. I wrote a big freaking check.

TEDDY. And he has helped many poor people in the fields of lawn care and pool maintenance.

SEAMUS. What about family?

TEDDY. Tyler doesn't speak to his family.

SEAMUS. Friends?

TEDDY. It's Hollywood. Don't use the "f" word.

SEAMUS. What about his wife?

TEDDY. Sheri? Why should he help her? *(Lights up on Sheri, wearing a robe. Memory moment. Tyler is younger, less jaded.)*

SHERI. Can I help?

TYLER. Oh, hi, honey.

SHERI. It's three A.M.

TYLER. I'm too psyched to sleep. I can't believe I got the part. Richard the Third. Live theater!

SHERI. I'm so happy for you.

TYLER. Live theater is what it's all about. REAL acting.

SHERI. You're gonna be great.

TYLER. It's just regional. Small house. I mean, it's not Broadway or anything.

SHERI. Don't downplay it, Jake. This is a turning point. I can feel it.

TYLER. How?

SHERI. I don't know. Sometimes you just trust in something bigger than yourself.

TYLER. They say all it takes is one break. Somebody sees you. You get an agent … Ha. Me with an agent, right? "Hello, this is Jake's agent. He can't come to the phone right now." *(Sheri, playing along, dabs his forehead with her bathrobe.)*

SHERI. Let me mop your brow, Mr. Steinberg.

TYLER. Haha! Can you imagine?

SHERI. *(Tenderly.)* I can imagine anything for you.

TYLER. Us. *(They kiss.)*

SHERI. Come on. Let's celebrate. *(She holds out her hand, then turns and Exits. Tyler follows her, then spins back to the present.)*

TYLER. *(To Seamus.)* Can we go now? They're probably seating people already! *(Another train sound. Teddy looks up.)*

SEAMUS. *(Nodding up.)* He likes the sound.

TEDDY. God likes the sound of a train?

SEAMUS. Aye. The sound that connects here to there.

TYLER. Can we PLEASE GO? From HERE to THERE?

SEAMUS. One more detail.

TYLER. Oh, come on! He told you who I helped. What else is there?

SEAMUS. Who have you hurt? *(Tyler snorts. Doesn't answer. He glances at Teddy. Gives him a "Well? Get me out of this" look.)* Who have you hurt?

TEDDY. *(Stepping up.)* Hurt? Why, my client wouldn't hurt a fly. He's the most considerate actor his directors have ever worked with and he —

SEAMUS. Who has he hurt?

TEDDY. How much time you got? *(Another rumbling sound. Kyle Morgan tumbles through the chute, wearing sweat pants and a sleeveless T-shirt. Tyler and Teddy step closer.)* It's Kyle Morgan!

TYLER. Where's a bouncer when you need one?

TEDDY. He died, too? *(Kyle groans, writhes on the floor.)*

KYLE. Unnnh … arrgggh …

TYLER. Even now he's over-acting. *(Seamus lifts the water glass but Tyler grabs it from him.)* Ah-ah-ah … Allow me. *(He delights in splashing it in Kyle's face.)* Welcome to your second act, Morgan.

KYLE. *(Coming to.)* Johnes? … Where the hell am I?

SEAMUS. It's a wee bit complicated, sonny. *(Kyle looks up into Seamus' face.)*

KYLE. Santa? *(He spots Teddy.)* Teddy?

TEDDY. Hello, Kyle. Long time.

KYLE. Will somebody please explain why I'm on my ass?

TYLER. Because there IS a God. *(Teddy helps him to his feet.)*

TEDDY. Kyle, think hard. What is the last thing you remember?

KYLE. I came home from Hailey's.

TEDDY. YOU were in Hailey's? WE were in Haileys!

KYLE. I didn't see you.

TYLER. We sat in the no-assholes section.

TEDDY. What did you eat, Kyle?

KYLE. Who the hell remembers? That crab on a stick thing, I think.

TEDDY. The "Tower of Shellfish"?

KYLE. Yeah …

TEDDY. I ate that! Tyler ate that! Kyle ate that! Voila! It must have been poisoned! Someone in Hollywood wanted us dead!

KYLE. Dead? What are you talking about?

SEAMUS. Well, Sonny …

TYLER. *(Stopping him.)* Uh-uh-uh. *(He motions slyly for Kyle to come closer. Kyle does. In Irish accent:)* You died. You passed over. This is where you wait. Feel for your heartbeat. You'll see. *(The three of them wait and watch for his reaction. He touches his chest. He tries to take it in. Finally, stunned …)*

KYLE. *(Meekly.)* But I have the Oscars tonight.

SEAMUS. Another one with the Oscars.

TYLER. He's not coming with us!

KYLE. But I'm nominated!

SEAMUS. *(To Kyle.)* You're also nominated?

KYLE. *(Proudly.)* Best Supporting Actor.

TEDDY. Don't you read the trades? They were in the same movie.

KYLE. *The Wind and the Fury.*

SEAMUS. Wait. You were a Civil War courier with a bad leg, bad eye and a speech impediment?

KYLE. No, I was the Confederate bugle blower with hepatitis and one arm.

SEAMUS. This was some story.

TEDDY. War is hell. *(Lights change. Sounds of bombs and guns. A movie clip.)*

KYLE. *(Dropping into character, complete with one arm.)* Sergeant, the Yankees are hiding just over that hill! *(Mimics bugle sound.)* Buh-buh-buh-buhhhhh! *(Tyler pushes in front of him, hopping on one leg.)*

TYLER. *(With speech impediment.)* Captain! I have news from the front! Summon the soldiers! Summon the soldiers! *(They continue yelling over each other and the sounds of war, flopping as they are "shot," each one over-acting the other. When they are finally "dead," Tyler drops his hand over Kyle's face. Kyle throws it off.)*

SEAMUS. *(To Teddy.)* Did many people see this movie?

TEDDY. It's an art film. That would defeat the purpose.

TYLER. *(Popping up.)* Anyhow, time to go get my Oscar!

KYLE. You're going?

TYLER. Sorry, Morgan, cab's full!

KYLE. What do I do here alone?

TYLER. Try counting the wives you've stolen. We'll be back before you're finished.

KYLE. Look. I don't know what you're talking about or where I am or who ate what shellfish. But I don't have my car keys … and I don't have my wallet … and so nobody is going to the Oscars without me!

SEAMUS. *(To Kyle.)* Is this award important to you too, boyo?

KYLE. I'd give my left kidney.

TYLER. Nobody wants your organs up here, Morgan, despite your propensity for sharing them on earth. Teddy. Let's go. *(Tyler and Teddy move as if to leave. Kyle pulls out a gun.)*

KYLE. I'm not kidding, Johnes!

TEDDY. *(Panicked.)* Don't shoot! *S'il vous plaît!* *(Meanwhile, he runs behind Tyler, keeping Tyler between him and the gun as they move about.)*

TYLER. *(Amazed, to Seamus.)* Wow. You really *can* take it with you. *(Moving closer.)* What's with the piece, Kyle? Planning a drive-by at Barney's?

KYLE. I'll kill you, you prick!

TYLER. *(Laughing.)* Go ahead! Maybe I'll go someplace with booze. *(Another train sound. Kyle looks up and around.)*

SEAMUS. Sonny. The weapon is useless here. *(Kyle is confused. He points it at Tyler. Tyler makes a childish face. He points it to the ceiling and pulls the trigger. It just clicks. No bullet. He lowers it, in stunned confusion. Seamus takes it from him gently.)* I always hated these things. *(Suddenly, another loud rumbling sound, and a new body falls through the shoot. A young woman, buxom, beautiful, in tight pants. It is Serenity. She lands with a thump and, like the others, is slow to move. Her rear end sticks up in the air and wiggles sensually.)*

TYLER. We can go now. My date's here.

KYLE. *(Startled.)* Holy mother of God! *(Seamus clicks, Kyle flops, but Seamus is riveted.)*

TEDDY. It's Serenity!

SEAMUS. It certainly is!

TYLER. That's her name, old man.

TEDDY. I'll bet she ate the shellfish! *(Seamus goes for the seltzer bottle.)*

SERENITY. Uhhnn … uhnnn … *(With Teddy, Kyle and Seamus staring, her moaning grows even more sensual. They draw near, fascinated.)* Uhnnn … unnn … *(As Seamus goes to spray her, Teddy grabs his arm.)*

TEDDY. Wait. Don't interrupt. *(They watch another moment. Seamus finally spritzes her. Serenity snaps out of it.)*

SERENITY. … where am I?

TYLER. Rise and shine, honey. Time for the Oscars.

SERENITY. OK. *(She gets up and primps as if nothing happened.)*

TYLER. The perfect date.

SEAMUS. Jacob. I need to tell her where she —

TYLER. *(Scolding a warning.)* Uh-uh-uh! Not now! Later!

SERENITY. *(Cheerily, to Seamus.)* It's all right, Mister. I've woken up in strange bars before. Just tell me I didn't do something really *really* embarrassing. I'd just die! *(A beat from them all.)*

SEAMUS. Perhaps it can wait.

TYLER, TEDDY and KYLE. Yes. Yeah. Right …

TYLER. Serenity, say hello to Mr. Seamus. *(She waves.)*

SERENITY. Hi, Mr. Seamus.

TYLER. Nice Mr. Seamus is taking us to the Oscars!

SERENITY. Is he the limo driver!

TYLER. More like the travel agent. *(As Tyler continues, we hear the distant sound of a timpani drum roll; it grows louder as the conversation goes on.)* Here we go, folks. This is everything I've worked for! The envelope rips. My heart is pounding. Salvation lies in three little words …

SEAMUS. Gross, not net?

TYLER. "The winner is"! "The winner IS … " *(Racing around.)* "The winner is-the winner is-the winner is! "THE WINNER IS … " *(Races to Seamus.)* Come on, Master Leprechaun! Open that door! *(He sings.) This will be my SHIII-ning hour! (Serenity follows around behind him. Eventually, all join in this circle romp.)*

SERENITY. Are we coming back here for the post party?

TEDDY. That's pretty likely.

SEAMUS. All right then. Assume the position.

SERENITY. Which one? *(Tyler/Teddy/Serenity/Kyle all drop to their knees. As if just noticing:)* Hey. It's Kyle Morgan! Hi, Kyle!

KYLE. Hello.

SERENITY. I love your work.

KYLE. Really? Which is your favorite —

TYLER. SHUT UP AND CONCENTRATE! I'm going to the Oscars! Say it loud, say it proud!

TEDDY. I'm going to the Oscars.

TYLER. I'm going to the Oscars!

SERENITY. I'm going to the Oscars!

KYLE. I'M going to the Oscars! *(Seamus emerges from behind the bar wearing a scarf and a hat.)*

SEAMUS. WE'RE going to the Oscars!

TYLER, TEDDY, KYLE and SERENITY. … We?

SEAMUS. Aye … *(Smiling.)* We. *(He flicks his hands up as the timpani drum roll reaches a crescendo with a cymbal crash. Blackout. Sound of train whistle.)*

End of Act One

24

ACT TWO

Music up. A song like Gene Autry's "Back in the Saddle Again."* As music fades, Lights up on Sheri, in her bedroom. She is half dressed in a gown, looking at a picture of Tyler. She is on the phone.

SHERI. Because it's the only place I can find him, that's why ... No, I can't get his address. When he moved out, I think he bribed every mailman in Los Angeles. And he doesn't call me back ... I know, I shouldn't call him all the time, I'm just ... I AM over him ... tonight, if I can give him the papers, I'm gonna ... *(She struggles with a pin, pricks her finger.)* Ow! ... You know, I do regret quitting the business before someone paid for my dress at least once ... *(A beat.)* No, no, I mean, I don't regret it. Those were crazy times ... *(As she continues, music rises, a campy, stirring, disco-like theme, suggesting danger and suspense. Enter Kyle, stage left, moving in exaggerated slow motion, dressed as a Chippendale stripper, wearing tuxedo pants, no shirt, and a bow tie.)* Kyle? ... No. That whole thing with Kyle was a big mistake ... *(Kyle points a gun at Sheri, dreamlike, then points in another direction, typical over-acted cop/buddy movie style. Sheri moves through his path as if he isn't there. He dives and rolls in ridiculous over-acting. Enter Tyler, wearing similar stripper outfit, a semiautomatic in one arm, a pistol in another. He, too, is in slow motion.)* Tyler was different ... Tyler was my husband ... still is my husband, technically ... No, he wasn't always a pompous ass ... *(Tyler is also doing gun poses, around Sheri, past Sheri. Then he and Kyle do exaggerated stripper-like moves on both sides of her, closing in.)* I know, but you should have known him before that Chippen-Cop stuff. He really wanted to be good and ... I thought we'd be together forever ... What? ... Oh, what always happens. He became a star, and the guy I knew disappeared ... Hold on, let me grab the other line ... *(She ducks and exits. Tyler and Kyle drop into exaggerated calisthenics, working their muscles and their egos.)*
KYLE. Good take, Sassy.

25

TYLER. Right back 'atcha, Morgan.

KYLE. Call me Sexy.

TYLER. Why?

KYLE. I called you Sassy.

TYLER. So?

KYLE. That's how it works. I called you Sassy, you call me Sexy.

TYLER. I don't want to call you Sexy.

KYLE. *(Chanting, kid-like.)* Call me Sexy. Call me Sexy. Call me Sexy.

TYLER. OK, OK! Good work … "Sexy."

KYLE. My Man!

TYLER. So where's the party tonight? AGENT! *(Enter Teddy, also in a silly, stripper-like outfit. And Serenity, who acts as a dresser. She helps Tyler put on formal wear as the dialogue continues.)*

TEDDY. You rang, Master?

TYLER. Can you hook us up tonight?

TEDDY. I believe that can be arranged.

TYLER. Lemme get out of something. Cell phone? *(Teddy reaches into his stripper pants, pulls out a cell. Teddy dials, then holds it up to Tyler's ear as Serenity continues to flirt with his body as he dresses. Lights up on Sheri.)*

SHERI. Hello?

TYLER. Hi, babe.

SHERI. Hi, Jake.

TYLER. It's Tyler, remember? You never know who's listening.

SHERI. We're on the phone, honey.

TYLER. They bug phones!

SHERI. OK. Tyler? I was thinking about what we talked about yesterday. *(Serenity has him distracted.)*

TYLER. Mmm. What's that, Sher?

SHERI. A baby? You know? How we can't wait any longer? I was even thinking of some names if we had a boy or a girl — I know, don't say it, it's stupid to even talk like that, it's just, I get so excited. Are you excited?

TYLER. *(Serenity all over him.)* Oh, yeah.

SHERI. I really want this, honey … Honey? … Are you there? *(He can barely answer.)*

TYLER. Uh-huh … Anyhow, I can't get home tonight. Got stuff to take care of.

SHERI. *(Disappointed.)* What stuff?

TYLER. Sher, if I had time to tell you what stuff, I could get it all done, right? I'll crash at Kyle's.

SHERI. Kyle lives three miles from us.

TYLER. You know traffic. Gotta run. Later. *(Teddy flips the phone shut. Lights off on Sheri.)* Free as a bird.

KYLE. Let's get crazy! *(They exit. Sheri alone in the light, back to where she began the scene. Music down.)*

SHERI. Anyhow, that feels like a long time ago … I will … of course I'll call … thanks … I love you, too. *(Beat.)* See me on TV? Yeah. I'll be the only one driving my own car. *(Lights down. Sheri exits, as crowd noise rises, then music up, a song like "Hooray for Hollywood."* A red carpet appears. Spotlights swirl across the stage. The Oscars are in motion. Enter Kyle, now in tuxedo, waving at assorted well-wishers.)*

ANNOUNCER VOICE. From *The Wind and the Fury*, it's Kyle Morgan. *(He waves, walks. Enter Tyler, Teddy and Serenity.)* From *The Wind and the Fury*, it's Tyler Johnes. *(More waving, walking. Teddy has a quick, furtive conversation with Kyle. Kyle exits. Finally, crowd noise down.)*

TYLER. This is great! Nobody knows we're dead!

TEDDY. Tyler. It's Hollywood. You only die at the box office. *(Working his Blackberry.)* Voila! We are up and running! Now I start a lawsuit against Hailey's and their goddamn shellfish! *(Tyler continues to wave at the crowd.)*

TYLER. Teddy, who cares at this point?

TEDDY. They kill me, I kill them back. And you should get those divorce papers signed. At least you keep half. Half the beach house. Half the Bentley. Half that Picasso in your bathroom. Your portfolio is worth a good twelve million.

TYLER. *(Still waving at people.)* And what'll I do with it?

TEDDY. Tyler. You know the game. Whoever dies with the most toys wins.

SERENITY. Tyler?

TYLER. Yeah?

SERENITY. Hi!

TYLER. Hi, Serenity.

SERENITY. Where's the old French guy?

TYLER. He's Irish, sweetheart.

TEDDY. I saw him by the water fountain, turning it on and off.

---

* See Special Note on Songs and Recordings on copyright page.

He was laughing like a hyena. *(Seamus enters, wearing a ridiculous formal tux from the nineteenth century. He is holding a glass of champagne, staring at it like a treasure.)*

SEAMUS. Some young woman handed me this drink. *(Confused.)* She asked "who" I was wearing.

TYLER. Say "Louie the Fourteenth."

SERENITY. It's an awesome tux.

SEAMUS. Thank you, dear. I wore this to my last formal event.

TEDDY. What was that?

SEAMUS. A hanging.

SERENITY. Cool!

TYLER. Isn't this great, Mr. Seamus? Just like I told you, huh? Watch this. *(He leans out as if making himself available to the crowd.)*

FANS. *(Offstage.)* We love you, Tyler!

TYLER. I love you, too!

SEAMUS. Do you know those people?

TYLER. Shit, no!

SEAMUS. But they love you?

TYLER. Good job I got, huh? … You know, Seamus. You never did mention what *you* did down here … on … solid ground.

SEAMUS. Oh. Well that was a long time ago. *(He can't take his eyes off the liquor. He admires it like a work of art. Tyler and Teddy exchange glances.)*

TEDDY. You gonna drink any of that, Poppi?

SEAMUS. Me? … Oh, no. I dare not. The rules, you know.

SERENITY. *(As if offering an important tip.)* Well, whatever you do, don't mix your booze with your meds. I did that once with extra strength Tylenol — I was so buzzed! *(Enter Kyle, racing in, wearing tuxedo.)*

KYLE. I don't believe it! I just got offered a part in the new Pacino movie.

TYLER. In catering?

KYLE. *(To Seamus.)* Can I take it? Please? It's only a six week shoot! *(Seamus looks down, as if the answer is no.)* Awww, this sucks!

SERENITY. Why are you asking him? *(To Seamus.)* Are you his agent?

SEAMUS. Oh no, my dear. I'm not his agent. Theodore is.

TYLER. WHAT?

KYLE. *(Caught.)* Who told you that?

TEDDY. *(Caught.)* It is preposterous!

TYLER. Teddy represents me!

SEAMUS. And Ass Clown.

KYLE. ASS CLOWN?

SEAMUS. Wanted someone younger, Theodore did. Hedge his bets. Been keeping it secret.

TEDDY. Honestly! The rumor mongering in this business has to stop!

KYLE. Yeah. Teddy and me? That's whack.

TEDDY. *Exactement!* It's whack! Put down that alcohol, Monsieur Seamus! It has gone to your head! Serenity, would you help Monsieur Seamus get rid of that drink! *(Serenity takes glass, and drinks the whole thing.)* That wasn't what I meant. *(He shoos her, and she leads Seamus off. Teddy pulls Kyle and Tyler together.)* While he is gone, I have been planning our escape.

KYLE. Escape?

TEDDY. *Certainment.* You don't think I'm going back to that nasty bar with the silly magazines. *Pfft.* He didn't even have peanuts.

TYLER. Didn't we make a deal?

TEDDY. So? We break the deal. I have my secretary tell Mr. Seamus "we piss."

KYLE. We piss?

TYLER. Pass, you moron. And we can't "pass" on dying.

KYLE. Why not? We say "we are going in another direction." Which is true, n'est ce pas? He goes there. *(Points up.)* We stay here *(Points down.)* When the time is right, we disappear. Are we agreed? *(They all put their hands in together. Tyler is last.)* Then I'll get to do the Pacino picture?

TEDDY. *(Mimicking Pacino.)* Hoo-hah!

KYLE. Awesome!

TYLER. *(Mocking.)* Awesome! *(Kyle squares off. He's had enough.)*

KYLE. Look, dude. What's your issue?

TYLER. *(Mocking.)* "Issue"? I don't have an "issue"!

KYLE. Then back off and let me win my Oscar.

TYLER. I can't believe I carried you through five Chippen-Cop movies!

KYLE. You? Who wants to see your saggy ass in a g-string?

TYLER. I'm winning that Oscar!

KYLE. When monkeys come outa my butt! *(As they grab each other, Seamus and Serenity enter upstage.)*

FAN. *(Offstage.)* Hey, Kyle! YOU'RE THE BEST, KYLE! YOU'RE

GONNA WIN, KYLE! We love you! *(Kyle enjoys this at Tyler's expense. He waves.)*
KYLE. Thank you.
FAN. *(Offstage.)* Can we get an autograph?
KYLE. *(Dismissive.)* Not right now.
FAN. *(Offstage.)* YOU SUCK! *(Tyler cracks up. From other side ...)*
FAN #2. *(Offstage.)* Hey, Tyler! Good luck, Tyler! We love you! TYLER! *(Now Tyler basks in it.)*
TYLER. Thank you. Love you, too!
FAN #2. Can we get an autograph?
TYLER. *(Trying to be nicer.)* As soon as we're finished tonight, if you come back, right here, I'll give you one, OK, sweetheart?
FAN #2. YOU SUCK! *(Enter Sheri.)*
SHERI. Kyle?
KYLE. *(Waving.)* Hey, baby!
TEDDY. Oh, great! *(Teddy runs in front of Tyler to hide him.)*
TYLER. *(To Seamus.)* Seamus! My WIFE? Can't I get a break in the afterlife?
SEAMUS. You wanted to see everything.
SHERI. *(To Kyle.)* Hi. I tried to call you around midnight. You didn't answer.
KYLE. Sweetcakes, the strangest thing happened.
TYLER. *(Disgusted.)* Sweetcakes? *(Seamus steps up.)*
SEAMUS. *(Offering hand.)* How do you do? My name is Seamus. *(Sheri is charmed but confused. She takes his hand.)*
SHERI. Hello. I'm Sheri.
SEAMUS. Did you used to be married to Tyler Johnes — with an H?
SHERI. *(Confused.)* Yes ...
SEAMUS. And now you live with Ass Clown?
KYLE. Enough!
TYLER. *(Jumping in.)* Hey. Look who it is! Hello, Sher!
SHERI. Jake?
TEDDY. Hello, Sheri.
SHERI. Teddy.
SERENITY. *(Innocently.)* Hiiii! I'm Serenity.
SHERI. *(She offers hand.)* I'm Sheri, Serenity.
SERENITY. Your last name is Serenity? That's my *first* name! *(Exchanged glances.)*
TYLER. So, isn't this cozy!

SHERI. Good to see you too, Jake.

TYLER. TYLER! CALL ME TYLER!

SHERI. Fine! Tyler, Jake.

TYLER. I thought you hated award shows — or was that before you mated with Doctor Dipshit over here —

SHERI. Oh God, not th —

TYLER. It's OK. I'll just scratch you out of my acceptance speech. Oh wait. You weren't in it!

KYLE. Hey, hey, chill, OK? I'm at the Oscars. I'm a NOMINEE. I don't have to deal with marital spats — especially when the people aren't really married anymore?

SERENITY. I'm thirsty. I'm going to the bar!

KYLE. Good idea. I'll go with you. *(They exit. Awkward beat. The spat is still in the air.)*

TEDDY. Ah. Isn't that Richard from Universal? Come, Monsieur Seamus. *(Pulling Seamus with him they exit. Tyler and Sheri are left alone, trying to get a footing on conversation.)*

SHERI. Nice company you're keeping.

TYLER. She's just a girl.

SHERI. Not the bimbo. She'll be history after tonight.

TYLER. More than you know.

SHERI. Hanging out with old Irishmen — now that's a new one. *(A beat. She softens.)* OK. In honor of the Oscars. Truce?

TYLER. Truce.

SHERI. How are you, Jake?

TYLER. Given the circumstances, my doctor would be impressed.

SHERI. Still staying out late, waking up in strange places?

TYLER. Aaa … little bit.

SHERI. You can't party forever.

TYLER. You're right. After tonight, I'm giving all that up.

SHERI. It's kind of strange, huh, you and Kyle in the same movie, and now up for the same award? How are you handling that?

TYLER. Fine, fine. My only concern is that he slept with most of the Academy.

SHERI. *(Laughing.)* That is possible.

TYLER. Do I detect a chill between you and Romeo of the lap dance?

SHERI. Stop it! Nothing happened that night you stormed out. For the millionth time: Kyle showed up drunk, looking for you, and passed out in our bed.

TYLER. Oh, and you just helped him take his clothes off.

SHERI. He did that himself. I think it's an involuntary reflex.

TYLER. Then you nursed him back to health.

SHERI. Actually, no. I spent the next few hours driving around trying to find my husband. But five minutes after I come home, he — you — shows up. And the rest is ... hysteria.

TYLER. I had every right to do what I did. What would YOU have thought —

SHERI. Please, Jake! You wanted out. It wasn't about Kyle. I almost wish it had been. *(Beat.)* Anyhow, didn't anybody tell you? I moved to Riverside. I start teaching next month.

TYLER. Riverside?

SHERI. I know. It's quiet, maybe a little boring, but this whole movie world was you, not me.

TYLER. Did Kyle do something to you?

SHERI. I didn't move because of Kyle. I've called you a million times.

TYLER. *(Lying.)* Really? Nobody told me ... So, you're here to root for Kyle or me? ... *(She begins to cross to him.)*

SHERI. Actually, I was hoping to see you. This may not be the best time, but ... *(She stops. She looks in his eyes. Something shifts.)*

TYLER. But what?

SHERI. Never mind. This is a big night for you. Damn it. *(She pulls away.)*

TYLER. Wait. *(Music starts. The Oscars are about to begin. Enter Teddy and Seamus.)*

TEDDY. Whoo hoo, that was fantastic! Oops.

SHERI. *(Tenderly.)* Call me tomorrow. *(She walks away quickly, torn.)*

TYLER. I'll be out of town tomorrow.

TEDDY. We'll be out of town tomorrow!

SHERI. So? They have phones, right? *(Sheri exits.)*

TYLER. *(To himself.)* Wrong. No phones. No cabs. No booze.

TEDDY. Forget about her, Tyler! Listen to this! I told Richard he never made a movie worth a pig's fart, and his wife was the ugliest creature to ever walk on two feet — or four! Ha! If I had known I was going to die, the people I could've told to piss off!

TYLER. Teddy, did you know Sheri wasn't with Kyle?

TEDDY. Of course.

TYLER. How?

TEDDY. Kyle said — maybe I heard it somewhere, someplace, I don't know.

TYLER. Why didn't you tell me?

TEDDY. Because it would only upset you, bubbelah.

TYLER. Don't call me "bubbelah."

SEAMUS. Do you still love this woman?

TEDDY. Tyler? He can have any girl he wants! She's the one who won't let him go. Calling him every other night. She is only after his money. *(To Tyler.)* Listen to me, Tyler. Wives come. Wives go. Movies are forever. You win this Oscar, it's immortality!

TYLER. *(Coming around to it.)* Yeah … you're right.

SEAMUS. Immortality, you say?

TEDDY. Oh, yes, Mr. Seamus. Wait until you see it!

SEAMUS. I've seen immortality.

TYLER. What's it like?

SEAMUS. Long. *(A beat. Music louder. Lights up on Serenity and Kyle, making out passionately. Tyler, Seamus and Teddy watch for a moment.)* Goodness!

TYLER. Getting one for the road, Morgan? *(Kyle and Serenity break apart, caught.)*

SERENITY. Sorry, Tyler. He told me he was dying.

TYLER. What'd you do to Sheri, you shit?

KYLE. Sheri? … I didn't do anything to Sheri. She's a great lady.

TYLER. You stole her from me, then you ditched her like some bimbo from the health club!

SERENITY. *(Slapping his face.)* That's awful! *I* go to a health club!

KYLE. *(Shaking it off.)* For your information, I didn't steal her from anyone. She was so sick of your colossal ego.

TYLER. MY colossal ego?

KYLE. *(As they close in on each other.)* And not that it matters, but me and Sheri was a real temporary thing, dude. She was just tired of her position with you.

TYLER. And you offered her a new position?

KYLE. *(Slyly.)* I offered her a couple. *(At this, Tyler attacks him, they grab and slap at each other as Teddy tries to break it up.)*

TEDDY. Stop it! These are the Oscars!

TYLER. You leech! You parasite!

TEDDY. Joan Rivers is watching!

TYLER. I get a real movie, you muscle in on it!

KYLE. Liar!

TYLER. I have a real woman, you muscle in on her!

KYLE. Liar! NOT THE FACE!

TYLER. Now you're trying to steal my agent!

KYLE. NOT THE FACE! *(They fall backwards, all on the floor, whipped.)*

TYLER. I can't even *die* by myself! Whadya do, bribe Hailey's for some of my poison shellfish?

KYLE. I didn't even know you were in that stupid restaurant! I was there with Sheri!

TYLER. *(Panting.)* Sheri? ...

KYLE. She was telling me about some new guy she's seeing ... some pharmacist or something ...

TYLER. Why is she telling you about some guy —

KYLE. Because she wants to marry him! *(Tyler is stunned, still trying to catch his breath.)*

TYLER. Marry him? ... *(Lights down on Kyle and Serenity. Enter Sheri, in wedding clothes. Wedding music up. She and Tyler embrace and dance in a memory moment. Teddy waves. Tyler waves back. Music down. Dance ends.)*

SHERI. Honey, aren't you going to introduce us?

TYLER. Oh, yeah. I forgot. Ahem. May I present my new wife, Sheri. Sheri, my new agent, Teddy LePetite. A giant in the business.

TEDDY. *Enchante,* madame. And congratulations. You have just married a man on the move. He will be large, eh? He will be a bright new star in the movie universe!

SHERI. *(Jokingly.)* How's he going to be as a husband?

TEDDY. Oh-hoo, that is not my department, n'est ce pas?

TYLER. Are you kidding? I'm gonna be husband of the year. I'm gonna win the Oscar for Best Supporting Spouse!

SHERI. *(Happy.)* We need to take some pictures with my family, honey.

TYLER. Wait, just listen to this. Tell her, Teddy. Talk about a wedding present!

TEDDY. It's a new action film. Big budget. Two police officers, undercover, as — oh, I love this! — as *strippers.* Ah? Ah-ah? Magnifique, yes? Undercover, but *no cover!* It's a little tweest.

TYLER. Teddy says it's six figures. I play one of the cops.

SHERI. *(Less than thrilled.)* That's wonderful, Jake. A little ... tweest.

TYLER. It starts shooting next month. House payment *(Claps*

34

hands.) taken care of!

SHERI. Don't you start that play next month?

TEDDY. Tsk tsk. That is what Teddy LaPetite is for! To get you *into* the right things and *out* of the wrong ones!

SHERI. We need to take those pictures, Jake.

TEDDY. Tyler.

SHERI. I'm sorry?

TEDDY. His name from now on: Tyler Johnes. With an h! J-o-h-n-e-s.

TYLER. What do you think, Sher? *(He strikes pose.)* Tyler Johnes. With an H. What do you think? … *(Sheri, puzzled, backs away.)* What do you think? … *(Sheri exits. Tyler looks after her. Blackout.)*

ANNOUNCER VOICE. *(Offstage.)* Welcome, ladies and gentlemen, to the eightieth annual Academy Awards, live from the Kodak Theater in Hollywood, California … *(Music louder. Searchlights crisscross the stage. When lights come back up, Tyler, Teddy, Seamus, Serenity and Kyle are seated. Seamus is next to Tyler, who is next to Kyle. On the other side is Teddy, next to Serenity. Music lowers to background.)* The nominees for Best Sound Editing … *(The following conversations are in loud whispers, with a shift after each announcer interruption.)*

SERENITY. I hate this category.

TEDDY. A waste of time.

SERENITY. Is Tyler gonna win?

TEDDY. Tyler … or Kyle.

ANNOUNCER VOICE. The nominees for Best Cinematography …

TYLER. Who's she want to marry?

KYLE. I told you. Some pharmo-dude!

TYLER. What's his name?

KYLE. How the hell should I know?

ANNOUNCER VOICE. The nominees for Best Costume Design …

SERENITY. Kyle is nice. Tyler's ex is pretty.

TEDDY. She's a ballbuster.

SERENITY. *(Sudden new voice.)* And Kyle, being younger, has greater earnings potential and more high profile media opportunities. He's kind of vacuous, but then, he's an actor.

TEDDY. Ah, oui … WHAT?

ANNOUNCER VOICE. The nominees for Best Foreign Film …

TYLER. Why was she telling you?

KYLE. Bro. She's moved on.

TYLER. How can she move on? She hasn't got my money yet!

KYLE. Will you shut up! *(At this point, Seamus appears to be asleep.)*

ANNOUNCER VOICE. Coming up, the awards for Best Screenplay, Best Adapted Screenplay, and Best Supporting Actor … *(Music rises, then drops out. Teddy leans forward and massages Tyler's shoulders.)*

TEDDY. Won't be long now.

TYLER. Yeah … Hey, Seamus — *(No response.)* Hey. Hey, old man? *(He jostles him. Nothing.)* Seamus? … Hey. Pssst. Teddy!

TEDDY. What?

TYLER. I think we have a dead dead man here!

TEDDY. What?

TYLER. He's not moving.

KYLE. *(Leaning in.)* What's going on?

TEDDY. The old man is comatose.

SERENITY. I bet he mixed his booze and his meds.

KYLE. Wait a minute! If he's gone — then we can stay!

TYLER. You're such an opportunist!

TEDDY. No, no, Kyle is correct! Death at the Oscars nullifies the contract. Monsieur Seamus … is in breach!

KYLE. Fuck breach. I'm changing seats.

TYLER. Right. God won't find you in the mezzanine.

KYLE. You know, when I win that Oscar, I'm gonna thank you for teaching me what NOT to become. And when you go to your stupid little bar with your stupid little leprechaun, why don't you ask him how you got in *The Wind and the Fury* in the first place. Ask him about the package deal … Or ask Teddy.

TYLER. Go to hell.

KYLE. Bite me, loser.

TYLER. Where do you get your material, gym class? *(Kyle takes off. Serenity rises.)*

SERENITY. I, uh … have to use the little girls room. *(She exits.)*

TEDDY. Tyler, I must advise you to consider this option.

TYLER. What? Ditch him?

TEDDY. It's a loophole.

TYLER. What if he's sick?

TEDDY. How can he be sick — He lives on a fucking cloud! Tyler. Listen to me, *maintenant*. We have made a lot of money together. And if you want to KEEP making money, you will lose this old fart and get out of here now. *(Tyler thinks.)*

TYLER. No.

TEDDY. *(Turning to sneak out.)* Suit yourself.

TYLER. Teddy. What did Kyle mean about how I got in the film?

TEDDY. Tyler, not now —

TYLER. You did a package deal? I was the throw in?

TEDDY. Tyler. I am your agent!

TYLER. And who else's?

TEDDY. Where is your gratitude? I made your life a thousand times better. *(A sudden spotlight on Tyler.)*

TYLER. Oh, God, not the cameras. *(Tyler pushes Seamus up, but he falls back into his lap, his head in his crotch. Teddy runs off. After Teddy:)* Hey! *(Another push. Another drop. Tyler must talk through smiling teeth.)*

SEAMUS. *(Still in his lap.)* Ahhhgh … ahhhrgh …

TYLER. Wake up Seamus. This isn't funny!

SEAMUS. Arrrgh … achchcc … *(Finally, out of options, Tyler drags a limp Seamus downstage. Seamus coughing all the way. When they reach what is the outer lobby, Tyler props Seamus to a sitting position. He keeps coughing.)*

TYLER. *(Slaps his face lightly.)* Jesus, Seamus! I'm saying Jesus! Aren't you gonna click me? Come on! Snap out of it! *(Looks at watch.)* Shit! Wait here! *(He runs back to the door, pulls it open.)*

ANNOUNCER'S VOICE. Here to present the Oscar for Best Original Screenplay —

TYLER. I still got time. *(He runs back to Seamus. Enter Sheri, as if leaving. Tyler spots her.)* Sheri! *(She turns. Sees them.)*

SHERI. Jake? Oh, my God.

TYLER. Do you have any water? *(She rustles through her bag, pulls out a small bottle. Tyler opens it quickly and tosses it into Seamus' face. He immediately calms down and breathes normally.)*

SEAMUS. Ahhh … thank you, boyo … we have to get back … I'm drying up.

SHERI. Is he all right?

TYLER. *(Gently.)* He'll be fine. Give us one second. *(She steps back. Tyler runs to door, pulls it open …)*

VOICE. And I just want to thank my legal team, and my publicity team, and my Scientology class, and my — *(He runs back to Seamus.)*

TYLER. *(Angry.)* Are you *deliberately* trying to kill my buzz?

SEAMUS. Let her go, boyo.

TYLER. What?

SEAMUS. She's already lived with a might-have-been. Don't make her mourn for one.

TYLER. Sheri? I don't understand.

SEAMUS. You do. Let her out of your heart.

SHERI. *(Peering in.)* Is he all right? I can get security — *(Tyler rises to her.)*

TYLER. No, no. He's OK now ... Hey, look, Sher. *(He leads her away.)* I heard about your new guy.

SHERI. You did? How?

TYLER. Bozo the Stud told me. Kyle. He said he's, what, a drug dealer?

SHERI. A pharmacologist. Oh, Jake ... Look, he's not you, he's not endlessly witty and tirelessly entertaining, but he's solid and he's kind and he holds my hand and he tells me he loves me and he keeps asking "When can we have a baby?" ... and ... I want to give it a try. You know? Normalcy?

TYLER. Look, Sher ... I need to say something here. That whole thing with Kyle —

SHERI. I told you, nothing —

TYLER. Happened. I know. I guess I always knew.

SHERI. Then why did you...? Jake, you ran around on me. I waited so many nights —

TYLER. I know. I know everything I did ... I'm ... sorry. *(Long beat.)* Sher. All this time you've been calling me? I didn't call back because ... it wasn't worth it ... *I* wasn't worth it. *(Beat.)* But this dope pusher —

SHERI. Pharmacologist.

TYLER. Right. He sounds like he can make you happy ... And that matters.

SHERI. That I'm happy? ... What about you?

TYLER. I've got the world on a string.

SHERI. You've got a girlfriend with a great ass.

TYLER. Same thing. *(A nice beat. They share a small laugh.)* You happen to bring those divorce papers? *(She removes them from her bag and walks to him.)*

SHERI. You can keep everything ... I never wanted the stuff.

TYLER. But Teddy said —

SHERI. Teddy's an agent —

38

TYLER. The beach house, the Picasso —

SHERI. Teddy's gross and net. Mostly gross —

TYLER. He said if anything ever happened to me — you would get everything.

SHERI. Jake? Snap out of it. Nothing's gonna happen to you. You're an Oscar nominee. *(He thinks for a second.)*

TYLER. Teddy says I'm worth twelve million.

SHERI. More like nineteen. The smartest thing you ever did was let me take care of the money. *(Tyler considers. Finally puts papers in his pocket.)*

TYLER. I'll put them in the mail myself. *(Beat.)*

SHERI. Thank you, Jake. For what you said. It's … kind.

TYLER. Sher, if I ask you something really off the wall, will you promise me you'll do it? No questions?

SHERI. *(Thinking.)* OK.

TYLER. Tonight, and every night for the rest of your life, say that prayer, "Now I lay me down to sleep."

SHERI. *(Joining in.)* I pray the Lord my soul to keep?

TYLER. That's the one.

SHERI. Why?

TYLER. I said no questions.

SHERI. But —

TYLER. Because sometimes you have to trust in something …

SHERI. … bigger than yourself? You remembered that?

TYLER. I'll remember everything.

SHERI. *(Softly.)* OK … *(Beat. They kiss. A sweet kiss somewhere between love and goodbye. He breaks it off with mixed emotions.)* See you around?

TYLER. Yeah … I'll be *(Motions to the air.)* … around. *(She smiles, begins to walk away. After her:)* Tell the pharmacologist I said "Hi." *(Sheri takes one last look at Tyler, then exits. Tyler watches her go. Seamus, on his feet now, has seen the whole thing. Tyler rips up the divorce papers.)*

SEAMUS. Do you know why God wants you to say it every night? "My soul to keep"? Because sharing your soul is how you know you have one. *(A roar of applause. Tyler looks at his watch. Panic. He runs, but Teddy and Serenity come racing out, intercept him.)*

TEDDY. Where did you go? Where did you go — you idiotic, OSCAR WINNING FOOL!

TYLER. Wha…?

SERENITY. I knew you could do it! My girlfriends said you were too old, but I told them I picked a winner!

TEDDY. What a maneuver! Disappearing! Making Kyle Morgan accept for you! It's brilliant! It's mysterious! It's like Brando with Pocahantas!

TYLER. Kyle accepted for me?

SERENITY. He ran down from the mezzanine —

TEDDY. — panting like a sonofabitch!

TYLER. Wait. I won? And I missed it?

TEDDY. Don't worry, I have it TIVO'd! Tomorrow, we'll watch it over and over! Whooee!

TYLER. Tomorrow?

SERENITY. Whip-eee! *(They start singing and dancing with each other.)*

TEDDY and SERENITY. There's no business like show business, there's no business I know … da, da, da, da, da, da, da … *(They freeze. Tyler looks over their heads to Seamus, who has straightened and grown more somber. He is standing on the second step of a staircase. He extends an arm.)*

SEAMUS. Ready to go, then?

TYLER. They don't remember they died.

SEAMUS. They didn't. You did. You had a heart attack. All by yourself.

TYLER. But why were they —

SEAMUS. You conjured them up. For company. They're back on their own paths now. Redemption, you do alone.

TYLER. But Sheri? Didn't I …

SEAMUS. Aye. You did good there. *(Tyler studies frozen Teddy and Serenity. He circles them.)*

TYLER. I don't know what to say to them.

SEAMUS. Tell them to stay away from shellfish. *(Teddy and Serenity snap out of it.)*

TEDDY. Whoa, whoa! Look at the time! The parties await! C'mon, stud!

SERENITY. C'mon stud!

TYLER. Just give me a minute, OK?

TEDDY. We'll see you in the stretch limo!

SERENITY. See you in the stretch limo!

TEDDY. Oh, by the way. This is yours. *(He hands the Oscar to Tyler.)* Haha! We're gonna get rich! *(Teddy exits. As Serenity shuffles away, she blows a kiss over her shoulder and wiggles her rear end. Tyler studies his Oscar.)*

TYLER. The Oscar. *(Beat.)* You're judged on your performance, you know.

SEAMUS. Aye. You always are. *(Tyler reexamines the statuette.)*

TYLER. This gonna be a long trip?

SEAMUS. Depends on traffic.

TYLER. We might get a lull?

SEAMUS. We might at that.

TYLER. You know, Seamus, you never did tell me what you did on earth.

SEAMUS. I was an actor. Terrible drunk. Couldn't keep my wig on straight. *(Beat. Tyler looks at his Oscar, puts it down on the ground.)*

TYLER. I could grab us a six-pack.

SEAMUS. You could try.

TYLER. Someone's always watching?

SEAMUS. Aye. *(He moves closer, hand extended, and Tyler finally grips it.)*

TYLER. *(Exhales.)* Aye. Aye … yiy yiy yiy yiy. *(As they move up the stairs, the sound of a train. Lights off on them, leaving a single spotlight on the statuette. Music up, the Mexican song "Ay, yi, yi, yi" ["Cielito Lindo"].)*

End of Play

41

PROPERTY LIST

Stack of magazines
Open chute on back wall
Seltzer bottle
Small clicker
Mirror on wall
Gun
Phones
White powder to look like cocaine
Business card
A Blackberry
Glass of water
Clipboard and pen
Scarf and hat
A pin or broach
Semiautomatic rifle
Pistol
Cellphone
Glass of champagne
Oscar statuette

SOUND EFFECTS

Harsh winds blowing
Man's deep breathing
Train
Scream
Loud rumbling sound
Sounds of bombs and guns
Timpani drum roll
Cymbal crash
Train whistle
Crowd noise

NEW PLAYS

★ **GUARDIANS by Peter Morris.** In this unflinching look at war, a disgraced American soldier discloses the truth about Abu Ghraib prison, and a clever English journalist reveals how he faked a similar story for the London tabloids. "Compelling, sympathetic and powerful." –*NY Times.* "Sends you into a state of moral turbulence." –*Sunday Times (UK).* "Nothing short of remarkable." –*Village Voice.* [1M, 1W] ISBN: 978-0-8222-2177-7

★ **BLUE DOOR by Tanya Barfield.** Three generations of men (all played by one actor), from slavery through Black Power, challenge Lewis, a tenured professor of mathematics, to embark on a journey combining past and present. "A teasing flare for words." –*Village Voice.* "Unfailingly thought-provoking." –*LA Times.* "The play moves with the speed and logic of a dream." –*Seattle Weekly.* [2M] ISBN: 978-0-8222-2209-5

★ **THE INTELLIGENT DESIGN OF JENNY CHOW by Rolin Jones.** This irreverent "techno-comedy" chronicles one brilliant woman's quest to determine her heritage and face her fears with the help of her astounding creation called Jenny Chow. "Boldly imagined." –*NY Times.* "Fantastical and funny." –*Variety.* "Harvests many laughs and finally a few tears." –*LA Times.* [3M, 3W] ISBN: 978-0-8222-2071-8

★ **SOUVENIR by Stephen Temperley.** Florence Foster Jenkins, a wealthy society eccentric, suffers under the delusion that she is a great coloratura soprano—when in fact the opposite is true. "Hilarious and deeply touching. Incredibly moving and breathtaking." –*NY Daily News.* "A sweet love letter of a play." –*NY Times.* "Wildly funny. Completely charming." –*Star-Ledger.* [1M, 1W] ISBN: 978-0-8222-2157-9

★ **ICE GLEN by Joan Ackermann.** In this touching period comedy, a beautiful poetess dwells in idyllic obscurity on a Berkshire estate with a band of unlikely cohorts. "A beautifully written story of nature and change." –*Talkin' Broadway.* "A lovely play which will leave you with a lot to think about." –*CurtainUp.* "Funny, moving and witty." –*Metroland (Boston).* [4M, 3W] ISBN: 978-0-8222-2175-3

★ **THE LAST DAYS OF JUDAS ISCARIOT by Stephen Adly Guirgis.** Set in a time-bending, darkly comic world between heaven and hell, this play reexamines the plight and fate of the New Testament's most infamous sinner. "An unforced eloquence that finds the poetry in lowdown street talk." –*NY Times.* "A real jaw-dropper." –*Variety.* "An extraordinary play." –*Guardian (UK).* [10M, 5W] ISBN: 978-0-8222-2082-4

DRAMATISTS PLAY SERVICE, INC.
440 Park Avenue South, New York, NY 10016 212-683-8960 Fax 212-213-1539
postmaster@dramatists.com   www.dramatists.com

NEW PLAYS

★ **THE GREAT AMERICAN TRAILER PARK MUSICAL music and lyrics by David Nehls, book by Betsy Kelso.** Pippi, a stripper on the run, has just moved into Armadillo Acres, wreaking havoc among the tenants of Florida's most exclusive trailer park. "Adultery, strippers, murderous ex-boyfriends, Costco and the Ice Capades. Undeniable fun." *–NY Post.* "Joyful and unashamedly vulgar." *–The New Yorker.* "Sparkles with treasure." *–New York Sun.* [2M, 5W] ISBN: 978-0-8222-2137-1

★ **MATCH by Stephen Belber.** When a young Seattle couple meet a prominent New York choreographer, they are led on a fraught journey that will change their lives forever. "Uproariously funny, deeply moving, enthralling theatre." *–NY Daily News.* "Prolific laughs and ear-to-ear smiles." *–NY Magazine.* [2M, 1W] ISBN: 978-0-8222-2020-6

★ **MR. MARMALADE by Noah Haidle.** Four-year-old Lucy's imaginary friend, Mr. Marmalade, doesn't have much time for her—not to mention he has a cocaine addiction and a penchant for pornography. "Alternately hilarious and heartbreaking." *–The New Yorker.* "A mature and accomplished play." *–LA Times.* "Scathingly observant comedy." *–Miami Herald.* [4M, 2W] ISBN: 978-0-8222-2142-5

★ **MOONLIGHT AND MAGNOLIAS by Ron Hutchinson.** Three men cloister themselves as they work tirelessly to reshape a screenplay that's just not working—*Gone with the Wind.* "Consumers of vintage Hollywood insider stories will eat up Hutchinson's diverting conjecture." *–Variety.* "A lot of fun." *–NY Post.* "A Hollywood dream-factory farce." *–Chicago Sun-Times.* [3M, 1W] ISBN: 978-0-8222-2084-8

★ **THE LEARNED LADIES OF PARK AVENUE by David Grimm, translated and freely adapted from Molière's *Les Femmes Savantes.*** Dicky wants to marry Betty, but her mother's plan is for Betty to wed a most pompous man. "A brave, brainy and barmy revision." *–Hartford Courant.* "A rare but welcome bird in contemporary theatre." *–New Haven Register.* "Roll over Cole Porter." *–Boston Globe.* [5M, 5W] ISBN: 978-0-8222-2135-7

★ **REGRETS ONLY by Paul Rudnick.** A sparkling comedy of Manhattan manners that explores the latest topics in marriage, friendships and squandered riches. "One of the funniest quip-meisters on the planet." *–NY Times.* "Precious moments of hilarity. Devastatingly accurate political and social satire." *–BackStage.* "Great fun." *–CurtainUp.* [3M, 3W] ISBN: 978-0-8222-2223-1

DRAMATISTS PLAY SERVICE, INC.
440 Park Avenue South, New York, NY 10016 212-683-8960 Fax 212-213-1539
postmaster@dramatists.com www.dramatists.com

NEW PLAYS

★ **AFTER ASHLEY by Gina Gionfriddo.** A teenager is unwillingly thrust into the national spotlight when a family tragedy becomes talk-show fodder. "A work that virtually any audience would find accessible." *–NY Times.* "Deft characterization and caustic humor." *–NY Sun.* "A smart satirical drama." *–Variety.* [4M, 2W] ISBN: 978-0-8222-2099-2

★ **THE RUBY SUNRISE by Rinne Groff.** Twenty-five years after Ruby struggles to realize her dream of inventing the first television, her daughter faces similar battles of faith as she works to get Ruby's story told on network TV. "Measured and intelligent, optimistic yet clear-eyed." *–NY Magazine.* "Maintains an exciting sense of ingenuity." *–Village Voice.* "Sinuous theatrical flair." *–Broadway.com.* [3M, 4W] ISBN: 978-0-8222-2140-1

★ **MY NAME IS RACHEL CORRIE taken from the writings of Rachel Corrie, edited by Alan Rickman and Katharine Viner.** This solo piece tells the story of Rachel Corrie who was killed in Gaza by an Israeli bulldozer set to demolish a Palestinian home. "Heartbreaking urgency. An invigoratingly detailed portrait of a passionate idealist." *–NY Times.* "Deeply authentically human." *–USA Today.* "A stunning dramatization." *–CurtainUp.* [1W] ISBN: 978-0-8222-2222-4

★ **ALMOST, MAINE by John Cariani.** This charming midwinter night's dream of a play turns romantic clichés on their ear as it chronicles the painfully hilarious amorous adventures (and misadventures) of residents of a remote northern town that doesn't quite exist. "A whimsical approach to the joys and perils of romance." *–NY Times.* "Sweet, poignant and witty." *–NY Daily News.* "Aims for the heart by way of the funny bone." *–Star-Ledger.* [2M, 2W] ISBN: 978-0-8222-2156-2

★ **Mitch Albom's TUESDAYS WITH MORRIE by Jeffrey Hatcher and Mitch Albom, based on the book by Mitch Albom.** The true story of Brandeis University professor Morrie Schwartz and his relationship with his student Mitch Albom. "A touching, life-affirming, deeply emotional drama." *–NY Daily News.* "You'll laugh. You'll cry." *–Variety.* "Moving and powerful." *–NY Post.* [2M] ISBN: 978-0-8222-2188-3

★ **DOG SEES GOD: CONFESSIONS OF A TEENAGE BLOCKHEAD by Bert V. Royal.** An abused pianist and a pyromaniac ex-girlfriend contribute to the teen-angst of America's most hapless kid. "A welcome antidote to the notion that the *Peanuts* gang provides merely American cuteness." *–NY Times.* "Hysterically funny." *–NY Post.* "The *Peanuts* kids have finally come out of their shells." *–Time Out.* [4M, 4W] ISBN: 978-0-8222-2152-4

DRAMATISTS PLAY SERVICE, INC.
440 Park Avenue South, New York, NY 10016 212-683-8960 Fax 212-213-1539
postmaster@dramatists.com www.dramatists.com

NEW PLAYS

★ **RABBIT HOLE by David Lindsay-Abaire.** Winner of the 2007 Pulitzer Prize. Becca and Howie Corbett have everything a couple could want until a life-shattering accident turns their world upside down. "An intensely emotional examination of grief, laced with wit." *–Variety.* "A transcendent and deeply affecting new play." *–Entertainment Weekly.* "Painstakingly beautiful." *–BackStage.* [2M, 3W] ISBN: 978-0-8222-2154-8

★ **DOUBT, A Parable by John Patrick Shanley.** Winner of the 2005 Pulitzer Prize and Tony Award. Sister Aloysius, a Bronx school principal, takes matters into her own hands when she suspects the young Father Flynn of improper relations with one of the male students. "All the elements come invigoratingly together like clockwork." *–Variety.* "Passionate, exquisite, important, engrossing." *–NY Newsday.* [1M, 3W] ISBN: 978-0-8222-2219-4

★ **THE PILLOWMAN by Martin McDonagh.** In an unnamed totalitarian state, an author of horrific children's stories discovers that someone has been making his stories come true. "A blindingly bright black comedy." *–NY Times.* "McDonagh's least forgiving, bravest play." *–Variety.* "Thoroughly startling and genuinely intimidating." *–Chicago Tribune.* [4M, 5 bit parts (2M, 1W, 1 boy, 1 girl)] ISBN: 978-0-8222-2100-5

★ **GREY GARDENS book by Doug Wright, music by Scott Frankel, lyrics by Michael Korie.** The hilarious and heartbreaking story of Big Edie and Little Edie Bouvier Beale, the eccentric aunt and cousin of Jacqueline Kennedy Onassis, once bright names on the social register who became East Hampton's most notorious recluses. "An experience no passionate theatergoer should miss." *–NY Times.* "A unique and unmissable musical." *–Rolling Stone.* [4M, 3W, 2 girls] ISBN: 978-0-8222-2181-4

★ **THE LITTLE DOG LAUGHED by Douglas Carter Beane.** Mitchell Green could make it big as the hot new leading man in Hollywood if Diane, his agent, could just keep him in the closet. "Devastatingly funny." *–NY Times.* "An out-and-out delight." *–NY Daily News.* "Full of wit and wisdom." *–NY Post.* [2M, 2W] ISBN: 978-0-8222-2226-2

★ **SHINING CITY by Conor McPherson.** A guilt-ridden man reaches out to a therapist after seeing the ghost of his recently deceased wife. "Haunting, inspired and glorious." *–NY Times.* "Simply breathtaking and astonishing." *–Time Out.* "A thoughtful, artful, absorbing new drama." *–Star-Ledger.* [3M, 1W] ISBN: 978-0-8222-2187-6

DRAMATISTS PLAY SERVICE, INC.
440 Park Avenue South, New York, NY 10016 212-683-8960 Fax 212-213-1539
postmaster@dramatists.com www.dramatists.com